Date: 4/11/14

J BIO LINCOLN
Mara, Wil.
Abraham Lincoln /

Abraham Lincoln

by Wil Mara

Content Consultant

Nanci R. Vargus, Ed.D.
Professor Emeritus, University of Indianapolis

Reading Consultant

Jeanne M. Clidas, Ph.D.
Reading Specialist

Children's Press®
An Imprint of Scholastic Inc.
New York Toronto London Auckland Sydney
Mexico City New Delhi Hong Kong
Danbury, Connecticut

Library of Congress Cataloging-in-Publication Data
Mara, Wil.
  Abraham Lincoln/by Wil Mara.
    pages cm. — (Rookie biographies)
  Includes index.
  ISBN 978-0-531-21058-1 (library binding) — ISBN 978-0-531-24979-6 (pbk.)
1. Lincoln, Abraham, 1809-1865—Juvenile literature. 2. Presidents—United States—
Biography—Juvenile literature. I. Title.

E457.905.M32 2014
973.7092—dc23[B]   2013034809

Produced by Spooky Cheetah Press
Poem by Jodie Shepherd
Design by Keith Plechaty

© 2014 by Scholastic Inc.

1 2 3 4 5 6 7 8 9 10 R 23 22 21 20 19 18 17 16 15 14

Photographs © 2014: Alamy Images/Don Smetzer: 8; Art Resource/bpk, Berlin:
31 top; Corbis Images/Bettmann: 3 top left, 27; Dreamstime/Indy2320: 4, 30 left;
Getty Images/George Eastman House: 19; iStockphoto/russellmcbride: 28; Library
of Congress: 12 (John Chester Buttre), 15 (Von Schneidau), cover, 20, 23, 30
right; Shutterstock, Inc./Critterbiz: 3 bottom; Superstock, Inc.: 31 center bottom
(Exactostock), 11, 24, 31 bottom; The Art Archive at Art Resource/Culver Pictures: 16,
31 center top; Thinkstock/iStockphoto: 3 top right.

Maps by XNR Productions, Inc.

Table of Contents

Meet Abraham Lincoln

Abraham Lincoln was the 16th president of the United States. His nickname was "Honest Abe." Abe led the American people through some very difficult times. He is thought of as one of the greatest presidents in U.S. history.

Abe grew his famous beard after he was elected president.

Abe was born on a farm in Kentucky on February 12, 1809. His family was very poor. The Lincolns moved to Indiana in 1816. Then, when Abe was nine, his mother died. His father married a woman named Sarah Johnston. Abe and his stepmother became very close.

Abe was born in Hodgenville, Kentucky.

This is a re-creation of the house where Abe lived from the ages of 7 to 21.

Abe grew to be tall and strong. He was a hard worker and loved to learn new things. Sarah taught him that he could do this by reading. Abe had only about one year of formal schooling, but he read so much on his own that he became very smart.

FAST FACT!

Young Abe also loved to wrestle. He got into hundreds of wrestling matches as a young man—and lost only once.

Working Toward the Presidency

Abe left home when he was 21. He worked at many jobs. He split rails to make fences and cabins. He ran a post office. He was even in the army. Through it all, Abe read a lot of books to teach himself new things.

FAST FACT!

Abe grew to be six feet four inches tall. He was the tallest president in American history.

11

Mary and Abe are shown here with three of their sons (*l to r*): Willie, Robert, and Tad.

One of the things Abe taught himself about was the law. A law is a rule that everyone has to follow. Abe became a **lawyer**. He gave people advice about the law and spoke for them in court.

Abe married a woman named Mary Todd in 1842. They would have four sons together. Sadly, three of them died before they became adults.

Abe also became a **politician**. He became very good at giving speeches. Soon, many people were coming to hear him. They liked him because he seemed very kind. He could also be funny. And he was good at telling stories.

This photo was taken when Abe was about 45 years old.

15

Abe often gave speeches about slavery. **Slavery** is when one person owns another person. Abe felt that slavery was wrong. He believed that all people in the United States should be free.

FAST FACT!

Abe wrote down ideas for his speeches on little pieces of paper. Instead of carrying his notes in his pockets, Abe stuffed them inside his tall black hat.

In 1860, Abe was elected president of the United States. The president is the most important politician in the country. Many people in the South were angry when Abe was elected. They were afraid he would try to end slavery. Abe said he would not try to end slavery in the South, but he would not let it spread to other states.

This illustration shows Abe being sworn in as president.

The Civil War

By 1861, eleven states in the South had left the United States. They called their new country the Confederate States of America. The U.S.A. was called the Union. The Union fought the Confederates to keep them from dividing the nation.

During the war, President Lincoln often visited Union soldiers in the field.

This photo was taken after President Lincoln gave his Gettysburg Address.

The Civil **War** dragged on for four years. Thousands of people died or were wounded. President Lincoln decided that if the Union won the war, he would end slavery throughout the land.

FAST FACT!

Lincoln gave a speech called the Gettysburg Address during the Civil War. It became very famous. He said the war was a fight to keep America together as one country—a country that believed *all* people were created equal.

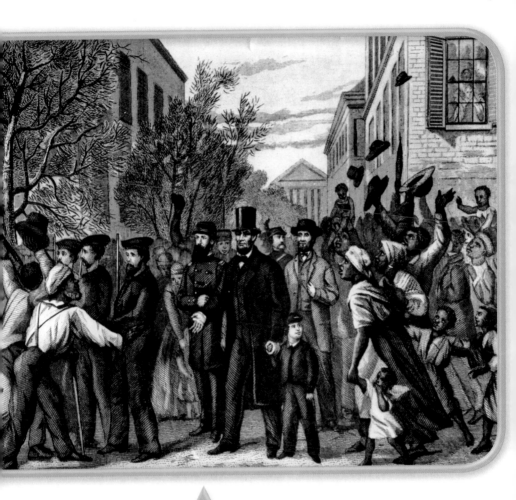

The president visited Richmond, Virginia, after the war. Former slaves cheered him. They were grateful to be free.

Let Freedom Ring

In 1865, the president worked to pass a law that made slavery illegal throughout the United States. In April of that year, the war finally ended. The Southern states were part of the United States again. And slaves were finally free.

Many people from the South were angry that they had lost the war. They were angry that the slaves were now free. One such person was an actor named John Wilkes Booth. He shot Abe Lincoln on April 14, 1865. The president died early the next day.

People across the country came to see Lincoln's coffin carried from Washington, D.C., to his home in Illinois.

Timeline of Abraham Lincoln's Life

1842
marries Mary Todd

1809
born in Kentucky

1846
elected to U.S. House of Representatives

As president, Abe Lincoln held the United States together and put an end to slavery. He will always be remembered as one of the greatest men in American history.

1860
elected to first
term as president

1865
killed by John
Wilkes Booth

1864
elected to second
term as president

A Poem About Abraham Lincoln

Half slave and half free, the country could not be.

So Lincoln fought for unity—and for emancipation.

And that is why today, many people say

he was among the greatest men to ever lead our nation.

You Can Be a Leader

- Read books to learn more about things that interest you.

- Take time to get to know people who are different from you.

- Tell your parents, teacher, or another trusted adult if you see someone being treated unfairly.

Glossary

lawyer (LAW-yer): someone who works in the business of making and upholding laws

politician (pol-ih-TISH-an): someone who helps to run a town, state, or country

slavery (SLAYV-er-ee): a system in which one person is owned by another person

war (WAR): a fight between two groups of people

Index

Facts for Now

Visit this Scholastic Web site for more information on Abraham Lincoln:
www.factsfornow.scholastic.com
Enter the keywords **Abraham Lincoln**

About the Author

Wil Mara is the award-winning author of more than 140 books. Many are educational titles for children.